CW00556512

G

CENGAGE Learning

Shakespeare for Students, Second Edition, Volume 1

Project Editor
Anne Marie Hacht

Rights Acquisition and Management
Lisa Kincade, Robbie McCord, Lista Person, Kelly Quin, and Andrew Specht

Manufacturing
Rita Wimberley

Imaging
Lezlie Light

Product Design
Pamela A. E. Galbreath and Jennifer Wahi

Vendor Administration
Civie Green

Product Manager
Meggin Condino

LIBRARY OF CONGRESS CATALOGING-IN-PUBLICATION DATA

Shakespeare for students: critical interpretations of Shakespeare's plays and poetry.-2nd ed. / Anne Marie Hacht, editor; foreword by Cynthia Burnstein.

p. cm.

Includes bibliographical references and index.

ISBN-13: 978-1-4144-1255-9 (set)
ISBN-10: 1-4144-1255-X (set)
ISBN-13: 978-1-4144-1256-6 (v. 1)
ISBN-10: 1-4144-1256-8 (v. 1)
[etc.]

1. Shakespeare, William, 1564–1616—Outlines, syllabi, *etc.* 2. Shakespeare, William, 1564–1616—Criticism and interpretation. 3. Shakespeare, William, 1564–1616—Examinations-Study guides. I. Hacht, Anne Marie.

PR2987.S47 2007

822.3'3—dc22 2007008901

ISBN-13
978-1-4144-1255-9 (set)
978-1-4144-1256-6 (vol. 1)
978-1-4144-1258-0 (vol. 2)
978-1-4144-1259-7 (vol. 3)

ISBN-10
1-1444-1255-X (set)
1-4144-1256-8 (vol. 1)
1-4144-1258-4 (vol. 2)
1-4144-1259-2 (vol. 3)

This title is also available as an e-book.
ISBN-13 978-1-4144-2937-3 (set) ISBN-10 1-4144-2937-1 (set)
Contact your Gale, an imprint of Cengage Learning sales representative for ordering information.

Printed in the United States of America

10 9 8 7 6 5 4 3 2 1

Henry IV, Part One

William Shakespeare

1596

Introduction

Henry IV, Part One continues the story Shakespeare began telling in *Richard II*. To fully understand the events of the later play, readers must know that in the earlier one, Henry IV, who was then known as Bolingbroke, returns from exile, has King Richard II imprisoned, and declares himself king. In *Henry IV, Part One*, Henry's former supporters, those who helped put him in power, join forces against him. Henry and his son, Hal, fight together against the rebels. The story continues in *Henry IV, Part Two*, with civil war still threatening the nation. At length, Henry IV dies and Hal becomes King Henry V.

Finally, in *Henry V*, the last of the group of plays known as the Lancastrian Tetralogy (Lancaster refers to the family, or house, from which Henry IV and Henry V were descended), Henry V conquers France, establishes peace, and marries Katherine, the French princess. Thus, the Lancastrian Tetralogy consists of *Richard II, Henry IV, Part One, Henry IV, Part Two*, and *Henry V*.

Scholars estimate that *Henry IV, Part One* was written and performed in late 1596 or early 1597. The play was first published in 1598 and in fact saw the publication of more quarto editions—seven before 1623's First Folio and two after—than any other Shakespearean drama. For the historical plot of the play, Shakespeare drew from several sources of English history that were written during Elizabethan times. His primary source was Raphael Holinshed's *Chronicles of England, Scotland, and Ireland* (2nd edition, 1586–87). Shakespeare also consulted Samuel Daniel's *The First Four Books of the Civil Wars* (1594), Edward Hall's *Union of the Two Noble and Illustre Families of Lancaster and York* (1542), and several other historical works. Finally, Shakespeare seems to have drawn heavily from an anonymous play, *The Famous Victories of Henry the Fifth* (1594?), for information on Hal's youthful escapades.

Regarding the reception of *Henry IV, Part One*, the character of Falstaff, at least, was being popularly quoted and referred to as early as 1598. That character's renown may have had something to do with the controversy that surrounded his name, as Shakespeare is understood to have been persuaded to revise the original performance name of Oldcastle. Scholars have determined that this change likely took place because descendants of the real-life Sir John Oldcastle, a religious figure from the early fifteenth century, bore relation to certain men who were sponsors of Shakespeare's troupe. Reflections on and comparisons between the real-life Oldcastle and the fictional Falstaff have been prominent in criticism of the play.

One of the major interpersonal conflicts in the play stems from Hal's strained relationship with his father. Henry IV is concerned that Hal is tarnishing his princely reputation with his association with the corrupt Falstaff and other common criminals. Falstaff is consistently associated with the idea of disorder, and his friendship with Hal appears to threaten the prince's ability to mature into a responsible ruler. Critics have argued over whether Hal, who after a confrontation with his father suddenly transforms himself into the prince his father wants him to be, was actually only using Falstaff to heighten the impact of his transformation. Hal's demonstrated affection for Falstaff has also been regarded as wholly sincere.

The main action of the play revolves around a rebellion against the Crown and one of its chief instigators, Hotspur. Hotspur's valor is admired by many, especially by Henry himself, who suggests to Hal that Hotspur would have perhaps been a more deserving heir to the throne. Given the complex characterizations of Hal and Hotspur, spectators and readers of the play are justified in wondering which of the two—if not another character entirely—should be viewed as the chief protagonist. As such, Hal's ultimate slaying of Hotspur may be seen as a heroic victory or as a tragic defeat. Regardless, the rise of Hal and the fall of Hotspur has been interpreted as symbolic of the evolution of English society from medieval times to the age of the Renaissance. In that respect, *Henry IV, Part One* may be the most monumental of all of Shakespeare's history plays.

Plot Summary

Act 1, Scene 1

At the beginning of *King Henry IV*, the king expresses his hope that a Crusade to the Holy Land will serve to preempt the civil strife that has been plaguing the English nation. However, the Earl of Westmorland announces that Sir Edmund Mortimer —who, in the context of the play, would have been heir to the throne had Henry IV not overthrown Richard II—has been taken in battle by Owen Glendower, a Welsh lord who has been wreaking havoc at the English border. Meanwhile, in fighting in the north, Sir Harry Percy, known as Hotspur, has taken as captives the Scottish lord Archibald Douglas and others—which confounds rather than delights Henry, as Hotspur's successes only remind him of his own eldest son's lack of accomplishments. Also, perhaps as influenced by his uncle, the Earl of Worcester, Hotspur intends to hold most of the captives for himself, rather than turn them over to the king. Henry sets aside his intent to commence a Crusade.

Act 1, Scene 2

In a tavern, Prince Henry, often called Hal, and Sir John Falstaff are exchanging remarks on the moon, the fortunes of thieves, and what Hal will do when he is king. Ned Poins then arrives to inform them of a chance for a robbery at Gad's Hill, near Rochester. Although he had just asked Falstaff about where they might "take a purse," Hal subsequently asserts that he is no thief and will not join them; Falstaff departs, leaving Poins to try and persuade Hal to go along. In fact, Poins proposes that they play a joke on their thieving comrades: after Falstaff and others commit the robbery, the disguised Poins and Hal will rob them in turn, specifically so that they can enjoy the excuses and lies that Falstaff will certainly provide afterward. Hal agrees to go along.

Upon Poins's departure, Prince Henry offers a soliloquy that is one of the most significant passages in the play. Comparing himself to the sun as obscured by clouds, he declares that he will soon expose and reform himself "by breaking through the foul and ugly mists." In that he remarks, "I'll so offend, to make offence a skill," he seems to be asserting that his associating with criminals is only part of a calculated plan to make himself appear all the more virtuous after his "reformation."

Act 1, Scene 3

King Henry is holding an audience with Sir Walter Blunt; the Earl of Northumberland; the earl's son, Hotspur; and the earl's brother, Worcester. After Henry scorns the offenses of the latter three, Worcester refers to the king's greatness as "portly" and as a "scourge," provoking Henry to dismiss him. Hotspur asserts that he had not explicitly and stubbornly refused to pass the prisoners along; rather, upon the close of the fighting at Holmedon, when he was physically and emotionally exhausted, a neatly dressed lord appeared, fresh, clean shaven, and perfumed, to demand the prisoners on King Henry's behalf. Thus, pained by his wounds and grieving over the killed soldiers, Hotspur immediately lost patience and could recall only that he responded "indirectly."

Blunt puts forth his belief that under the circumstances Hotspur's comments ought not be held against him, but Henry remains angered that Hotspur will not turn over the prisoners until the king offers a ransom for Mortimer, whose sister is married to Hotspur. The king then professes his belief that Mortimer had "wilfully betrayed" the men that he had led to death in battle—he notes as evidence that Mortimer married the daughter of Glendower, his supposed enemy—such that he should be considered a traitor and in no way deserved to be ransomed and brought home. Hotspur then cites reports of the extended battle fought by Mortimer and of the multiple wounds he received, but Henry simply refuses to believe these reports and again demands the unconditional delivery of the prisoners.

Left alone, Hotspur and Northumberland inform the returning Worcester of what has just taken place; Hotspur notes how the "ingrate and cankered Bolingbroke"—he uses the king's non-royal name to express his discontent—trembled at the name of Mortimer, whom Richard had indeed named as heir to the throne. Hotspur then expresses anger over the fact that his father, who in assisting Henry in attaining the kingship was essentially an accomplice to Richard's murder, should then be subject to "a world of curses" by the king. While his father and uncle try to reason with him, Hotspur speaks of revenge and gets carried away by his emotions. Eventually, Hotspur calms down and Worcester declares that they should free the prisoners, thus allying themselves with Scotland, and consult the Archbishop of York, who will wish to avenge his own brother's death at Henry's orders. Joining forces also with Mortimer and Glendower, then, they can all plot against Henry.

Act 2, Scene 1

At an inn yard in Rochester, two early-rising carriers are discussing their preparations for departure and the laxity of the ostler, or horse keeper, when Gadshill shows up to ask whether he might borrow a lantern. Suspicious, knowing the prominence of thieves in the area, the carriers refuse to give Gadshill even the correct time of day. When the carriers depart, Gadshill converses with the inn's chamberlain, who assists thieves by providing information about wealthy travelers—in this instance, about a company including a well-off landowner and an auditor. After asserting his honor as a thief, Gadshill assures the chamberlain that he will receive his share of the booty.

Act 2, Scene 2

On the road near Gad's Hill, Poins has hidden Falstaff's horse to provide the company of thieves with amusement. Indeed, Falstaff rails against Poins and declares his inability to walk anywhere at all in any comfort. Hal is ineffectually trying to calm Falstaff when Bardolph, Peto, Poins, and Gadshill arrive, with the latter informing the others of the travelers coming their way. Hal declares that he and Poins—who finally informs Falstaff of his horse's whereabouts—will seal off the escape route farther along the road, and they depart just before the travelers arrive. Falstaff and the others proceed to rob the travelers, only to be robbed in turn by the disguised Hal and Poins.

Act 2, Scene 3

At the home of the Percys, in Warkworth Castle, in Northumberland, Hotspur reads a letter from an anonymous lord who declines to take part in the Percys' proposed rebellion, citing the uncertainty of the effort. After affirming to himself the trustworthiness of the rebellion's major players, Hotspur dismisses the lord as "a frosty-spirited rogue" and "a pagan rascal"; he also first expresses, then negates concern that the lord will inform King Henry of their plot. Lady Percy, his wife, then arrives to chastise him for being so uncommunicative and solitary a husband and for focusing so much of his energy on warfare. Ignoring her inquiries as to why he has been especially preoccupied as of late, Hotspur asks a servant about preparations for his departure; growing enraged at Hotspur's stonewalling her, Lady Percy announces her suspicion that he and her brother Mortimer are engaged in some plot against King Henry. Hotspur then asserts that he does not even love his wife, as love is far less important than the political intrigue under-way—though he momentarily adds that he will later "swear / I love thee infinitely" but that he simply will not inform her of the plot, even though she will be joining him wherever he goes.

Act 2, Scene 4

At a tavern, presumably the Boar's Head, in London's Eastcheap district, Hal and Poins emerge from hiding to share in their amusement at their successful robbing of their companions. After boisterously discussing how he has just learned to drink with the peasant servers in the basement, Hal proposes a jest of his own: he will engage the server Francis in conversation while Poins summons him from the other room, such that they can provoke Francis to repeatedly utter "anon." Indeed, while Hal inquires about Francis's age and the price of sugar, among other ramblings, Poins repeatedly calls for service, and Francis parrots away as expected. When the vintner announces that Falstaff and the other thieves are waiting outside, Hal expresses his delight in participating in such playful activity while mocking the ever-industrious, Scot-killing Hotspur.

Upon entering the tavern, Falstaff rants and raves about nothing in particular, repeatedly declaring, "A plague of all cowards." As Prince Henry insists that Falstaff explain his consternation, Falstaff begins his tall tale about how he and the others were overtaken by a hundred adversaries after committing the robbery. Falstaff notes how he received various minor wounds (mostly to his clothing), in fending off these men, their number ever changing as Falstaff's tale continues; he pointedly mentions "two rogues in buckram suits," as Hal and Poins had been dressed in disguise. At length, Hal accuses Falstaff of lying, and the two comically insult each other; Hal then informs the company that he and Poins were actually the two men who had robbed them—at which revelation Falstaff asserts that he had known all along and had simply seen fit to leave the prince unharmed.

When the hostess enters to inform the prince that a nobleman has arrived to speak with him, Falstaff departs to send him away. Meanwhile, Peto informs Hal that Falstaff had compelled them all to hack their swords with their daggers and smear blood on their clothes in hopes of convincing Hal and Poins that they truly had fought valiantly before being robbed of their booty. When Falstaff returns, he relates the news he has learned: that Hotspur, Glendower, Mortimer, Northumberland, Douglas, and Worcester are plotting against the king, and that Hal will need to return to the court in the morning. In spite of the obvious peril, Hal insists that he is not afraid Falstaff, in turn, insists that Hal practices interacting with his father, whom Falstaff will impersonate, with a cushion as his crown, to the hostess's amusement. As Henry, Falstaff castigates Hal for his engaging in thievery and keeping such base company—excluding a "goodly portly man" whom he holds to be "virtuous." After Falstaff praises himself at length, Hal insists that they switch roles: the prince will play his father, and Falstaff will play the prince. As Henry, Hal seizes the opportunity to thoroughly ridicule the "fat old man" whose company he keeps—and Falstaff pretends not to know the person about whom Hal speaks. When Hal utters his name, Falstaff offers a comical defense of himself; nevertheless, Hal, as king, insists that he will still see fit to "banish plump Jack."

The tavern is thrown into commotion upon the arrival of the sheriff and "a most monstrous watch." After entreating Hal not to turn him over for his thievery, for which he would surely be hanged, Falstaff hides behind a curtain. Hal assures the sheriff that he will send the "gross fat man" to him the following day, and the sheriff departs. Falstaff is then found to have fallen asleep in his hiding place, and Peto extracts from his pocket a number of papers, one of which is a receipt showing that Falstaff had purchased a good deal of wine and a very small amount of bread. Letting his friend sleep, Hal declares that the stolen money will be repaid and that he will procure for Falstaff a position of command in the king's military force. Everyone then retires.

Act 3, Scene 1

Hotspur, Worcester, Mortimer, and Glendower are meeting to discuss specifics regarding their intended rebellion. When Glendower asserts that grand natural events occurred at the time of his birth, Hotspur iterates the Elizabethan belief regarding earthquakes: that they are caused by winds pent up within the earth escaping in an eruption. Glendower insists that his magical powers are unequaled on the isle of Britain—and further that he could teach them to Hotspur, who then insists that Glendower summon the devil.

Glendower eventually turns their attention to the map and their intended division of the country: with the Trent and Severn rivers serving as borders, the archdeacon has allotted the southeastern portion of the nation to Mortimer, the region of Wales to Glendower, and the northernmost region to Hotspur —who remarks that his share seems too small; likewise, Mortimer feels slightly cheated; as such, Worcester helps them agree to divert the river's course—but Glendower is opposed. Hotspur and Glendower resume arguing, now about the Welsh language, before Glendower finally concedes and departs. After Hotspur disparages Glendower and Mortimer defends him, Worcester chides Hotspur for his brashness.

Glendower and the wives of Hotspur and Mortimer then arrive, and Mortimer laments his inability to communicate with his Welsh-speaking mate and declares that he loves her and will soon learn to speak with her. Lady Mortimer then offers her husband a song, which she sings while Hotspur continues speaking coarsely to his wife, who tries to hush him. Hotspur goes so far as to chide Lady Percy for swearing such mild oaths before they all depart.

Act 3, Scene 2

Dismissing some attending lords, King Henry engages in a private discussion with his son, lamenting that his son had thus far so disappointed him with respect to the way he was living his life. The prince seeks pardon for his behavior, and the king goes on to point out the advantages a leader can reap by not allowing the common people to know him too well, pointing out how much Richard had lowered opinions of himself by consorting and even arguing with the masses. The king then invokes Hotspur, his son's peer, as a far better model of a princely warrior, as evidenced by his successes in battle; Henry even mentions his suspicion that his eldest son might rebel against him. The prince then declares that he will soon win his father's respect and his own honor by slaying Percy. When Sir Walter Blunt arrives to announce that Douglas, the Scot, had held counsel with the English rebels, the king notes that Westmorland and his son, John of Lancaster, have already departed for Bridgnorth, where they will engage the rebels in battle. Prince Henry, called Harry by his father, will travel there by a different route so as to collect more men.

Act 3, Scene 3

Back in the tavern, Falstaff asks Bardolph whether or not he appears to have lost some weight and claims that he will reform his ways. Bardolph mocks him, and so Falstaff in turn mocks his friend's red nose at length. When the hostess comes, Falstaff asks whether the person who picked his pocket has been identified; as the hostess responds negatively, Falstaff demands that he be reimbursed for valuables that had supposedly been in his pocket —until Prince Henry marches in to confirm that Falstaff had borne nothing valuable. Falstaff then begins subtly insulting the hostess, Mistress Quickly, who does not comprehend him, and Hal at last admits to having picked Falstaff's pocket. Hal then notes that he paid back the money that had been robbed and informs Falstaff of his commission at the head of a body of foot soldiers. Finally, the men all depart to soon meet the rebels in battle.

Act 4, Scene 1

At the rebels' camp, near Shrewsbury, Hotspur and Douglas are praising each other's qualities as soldiers when a messenger arrives to inform them that Northumberland is bed ridden with sickness and will not be able to join them; in addition, men who had been loyal to Northumberland could not be persuaded to go in his absence, severely reducing the rebels' numbers. Hotspur tries to rally their courage, but Worcester points out that even those rebels who have already joined them may be confused and disheartened by the untimely absence of one of their purported leaders. Nevertheless, Hotspur and Douglas express optimism. Yet Sir Richard Vernon then arrives to inform them that the king's forces are indeed on their way, in great numbers—with Prince Henry appearing especially daunting. Hotspur still declares his excitement over the coming battle with the royal forces and especially with the prince; however, Vernon also notes that Glendower will not be able to reach them in time for that battle, and Hotspur is left declaring, "Doomsday is near; die all, die merrily."

Act 4, Scene 2

Outside of Coventry, Falstaff sends Bardolph to fetch some wine. Falstaff then confesses in a prose soliloquy that he has been abusing his position as the head of a regiment by taking bribes, such that his collection of men was fairly pathetic and hardly battle worthy. Hal and Westmorland arrive to check in, with the prince calling Falstaff's men "pitiful rascals," then leave again to prepare for the coming battle.

Act 4, Scene 3

Back at the rebel camp, Hotspur thinks they should attack immediately, while Douglas, Worcester, and Vernon think that they should wait until they have secured supplies and their horses have all arrived and rested. Sir Walter Blunt shows up, representing the king, to inform them of his offer of full pardons and attention to their grievances if they will cease their rebellion. Hotspur recalls how his father had helped the king return to England from his exile, and how the king had gained the favor of the masses before executing supporters of the absent King Richard; at length, Hotspur details the ways in which the king had betrayed the very lords who had helped him attain his power. Still, Hotspur tells Blunt that Worcester will visit them in the morning in the interest of negotiating peace, with Westmorland to be held at the rebel camp to ensure Worcester's safe return.

Act 4, Scene 4

At his house, the Archbishop of York is dispatching Sir Michael to the rebel forces with urgent messages. The archbishop expresses to Sir Michael his fear that without Northumberland, Glendower, and Mortimer, the rebel forces will be soundly defeated—leaving the archbishop himself, a rebel supporter, in grave danger as well.

Act 5, Scene 1

At the king's camp, near Shrewsbury, the king and Prince Henry are greeting the day when Worcester and Vernon arrive from the rebel camp. After the king exhorts them to abandon their rebellion, Worcester insists that they had only fallen out of line because they had been so severely disrespected by the king himself. As Hotspur did before, Worcester details how the rebels had helped

Henry obtain the kingship and how he had come to oppress them afterward. The king denounces their complaints as hardly worth rebelling over, and Prince Henry offers to fight Hotspur man to man so as to resolve the conflict without mass bloodshed— but the king withdraws his son's offer and asks Worcester to simply bring his offer of pardons back to his comrades. Prince Henry expects that the offer will be refused by the confident Douglas and Hotspur, and everyone prepares for battle—Falstaff by explaining to himself the worthlessness of honor.

Act 5, Scene 2

Returning to the rebel camp, Worcester tells Vernon that he will not relay the king's offer to Hotspur and the others, as he believes that even if they receive the king's pardons, he will not truly forgive them and sometime in the future will intrigue against them. Indeed, Worcester tells Hotspur that the king has called them to battle, with no offer of mercy, and Douglas sends Westmorland back to the king with words of "brave defiance." Worcester then tells Hotspur of Prince Henry's gentlemanly challenge, and Hotspur again expresses his desire to meet the prince in battle. A messenger then arrives to tell them that the king's forces are on the way, and the rebels rally to fight.

Act 5, Scene 3

With the battle raging, Douglas happens upon Blunt, who is impersonating the king. Douglas tells of having already killed one of the king's doubles, Lord Stafford, and proceeds to kill Blunt as well. Hotspur arrives to tell Douglas that the man he has killed is not the king after all, and the two return to the fray. Falstaff appears, comments on the slain Blunt, and notes that he has led all but three of his men to their deaths. Prince Henry appears seeking to make use of Falstaff's sword or pistol, but Falstaff has only a bottle of wine to give him.

Act 5, Scene 4

The king implores Prince Henry, who is wounded, to return to their tents, but the prince refuses to leave the battle, as does his young brother John, who in returning to battle earns praise from Prince Henry. Douglas then comes upon the king and doubts his authenticity; the two fight, and Douglas gains the upper hand—but Prince Henry then storms in and fights Douglas until he flees, saving his father's life. When the king sets off, Hotspur arrives, and he and Prince Henry exchange words before engaging each other. While watching, Falstaff is set upon by Douglas; when Falstaff falls as if dead, Douglas immediately departs. Then, Hotspur, too, falls to the ground, mortally wounded, and laments his defeat before dying. Prince Henry praises the fallen warrior and shows his respect by hiding Hotspur's mangled face with a small piece of his battle gear.

Prince Henry then discovers Falstaff and laments his passing—but as soon as the prince departs, Falstaff rises and expresses how glad he is to have counterfeit his death so as to remain alive. Fearing that Hotspur, too, may still live, he stabs him in the thigh before hefting the body onto his back. When the two princes return, they express amazement at Falstaff's being alive, as Prince Henry had seen him dead. Falstaff then insists that Hotspur, too, had risen, and that they had fought for an hour before Falstaff killed him. Prince Henry expresses his indifference toward receiving the credit for Hotspur's death, and in departing Falstaff once again speaks of reforming himself.

Act 5, Scene 5

With the battle over, and the royal forces having proven victorious, the king scorns the captured Worcester for having failed to deliver the offer of pardon to the other rebels. The king then announces that Worcester and Vernon will be executed, while Prince Henry declares that the captured Douglas should be freed. To close the play, the king dispatches John and Westmorland to meet Northumberland, while he and Prince Henry will travel to Wales to strike at Glendower, so that the rebellion might be fully quashed.

Media Adaptations

- A television production of *Henry IV, Part I*, was directed by David Giles for the British Broadcasting Corporation in 1979 as part of "The Shakespeare Plays" series. A DVD collection of the entire series is available for purchase on the B.B.C. website.

Archibald, Earl of Douglas

Leader of the Scottish army, Douglas forms an alliance with the Percys, his former enemies, to rebel against King Henry IV; the Scot's interactions with Hotspur largely reflect their similar warrior-like characters. In the closing act, Douglas slays Sir Walter Blunt and nearly kills King Henry IV, but Prince Henry drives him off. Perhaps in that Douglas declines to interfere in Hal's battle with Hotspur, Hal suggests that the captured nobleman be freed.

Bardolph

One of Falstaff's thieving companions, Bardolph is depicted as even more of a coward and drunkard than the unruly Falstaff.

Sir Walter Blunt

Blunt is a nobleman who, with the Earl of Westmorland, leads King Henry IV's army. While the real-life Blunt was given little attention in historical records, Shakespeare molded him into an embodiment of honor: during the battle at Shrewsbury, when he is disguised as King Henry, he fails to inform Douglas that he is not the true king even when his death is at hand.

Earl of Westmorland

The Earl of Westmorland is a nobleman who, with Sir Walter Blunt, leads King Henry IV's army.

Sir John Falstaff

An irresponsible, merry, and often drunk companion of Prince Hal, Falstaff tempts Hal into a variety of mischievous deeds, but eventually loses his influence over the prince, as Hal accepts his responsibilities as heir to the throne. Falstaff is often called a tempter or a corrupting force; upon his first appearance, after he has uttered no more than "Now, Hal, what time of day is it, lad?" the prince launches into an invective against his gluttony, drunkenness, and general debauchery, leaving little doubt as to his character. Falstaff proves himself a coward on more than one occasion, such as when Hal and Poins beset his band of thieves after their robbery at Gad's Hill and when Falstaff leads his regiment to death at Shrewsbury but somehow escapes death himself. Falstaff never really denies his cowardice; rather, he frames it as the simple valuing of life over death, which any reasonable human being should choose.

Falstaff may justifiably be seen as the central character in *Henry IV, Part One*, as an aspect of almost every major theme is illustrated through his personality, and in particular ways he rests in distinct opposition to King Henry, Prince Henry, and Hotspur. In fact, Falstaff has more lines than any other character, with 585 lines, as followed by Hotspur (545) and Hal (535). In almost every scene in which Falstaff appears, he is literally and figuratively the center of attention, as demonstrated by conversational patterns and topics, and by the innumerable references to his girth.

With respect to the king, Falstaff serves as an alternative role model for Hal. Hal's private audience with his father features a series of longer speeches produced first by the king, then by the prince; that is, the king is essentially relating his perceptions to Hal, who respectfully receives them. Falstaff, on the other hand, is ever conversationally parrying with Hal, allowing the prince to actively develop and refine his own thoughts (even if they are merely comical ones), rather than leaving him passively absorbing information. The scholar Valerie Traub, for one, has posited that Falstaff in fact serves as more of a mother figure than a father figure in that he embodies certain qualities that Shakespeare denotes as feminine—such as cowardice.

With respect to Hal, then, Falstaff is effectively attempting to draw him fully out of the world of the court and join him in the world of thievery. In his introduction to the play, David Bevington characterizes the world Falstaff dangles in Hal's face as one of eternal immaturity:

> "Falstaff offers Hal a child's world in
> which he need never grow up, in

which even King Henry's most serious worries can be parodied in the comic language of euphuistic bombast. Falstaff's plea is for the companionship of eternal youth: sport with me, he says in effect to Hal, and let those who covet the world's rewards suffer the attendant risks."

Hal, of course, declines to lose himself in Falstaff's world of irrelevance, largely out of a sense of moral obligation to his father, to his country, and perhaps most prominently to himself.

Finally, with respect to Hotspur, Falstaff offers the extreme opposite of Hotspur's glorification of honor; Falstaff in fact utterly devalues honor through question-and-answer rhetoric, dismissing the notion as little more than a word. The sight of the slain Blunt leads Falstaff to remark, "There's honor for you." In general, then, Falstaff lies in opposition to what other characters hold as virtues; as such, Shakespeare's genius may be evident in the fact that Falstaff is portrayed not as a deplorable monster but as a lovable teddy bear, often placing the other characters' moral high ground in doubt.

Francis

Francis is a tapster, or server of wine, at the tavern. With the help of Poins, Hal subjects Francis to a prolonged jest, provoking him to repeatedly utter, "Anon, anon." Commentators have noted that

Francis's dilemma, being caught between two opposing forces (that is, customers), loosely mirrors Hal's dilemma, as he is caught between the two opposing worlds of court and tavern.

Gadshill

Gadshill is the "setter" among Falstaff's company of thieves, meaning that he obtains information about travelers from inns and relays that information to his companions on the road.

Owen Glendower

A Welsh soldier and ally of the Percys, he is reputed to have magical powers. He and Hotspur bicker during the rebels' division of what they hope to be the conquered English nation, as Hotspur denounces Glendower's powers as worthless superstition and empty claims. If Hotspur, with his undying devotion to soldierly honor, represents the medieval era, Glendower and his purported magic may be seen as representing the dark ages. Indeed, Glendower's Wales, where the women commit "shameless transformation" on the bodies of the defeated English soldiers, and where the language is ridiculed as savage by Hotspur, is depicted as less civilized than England.

King Henry IV

Formerly known as Bolingbroke, Henry, who won the crown through rebellion, faces the same threat of usurpation that he once posed. In the first scene of the play, Henry decides not to embark on a Crusade to the Holy Land due to the civil unrest in his kingdom. He had originally decided to undertake the journey at the end of *Richard II*, when he vowed to atone for the guilt he felt when Richard was murdered by Sir Pierce of Exton. Sir Pierce, an associate of Henry's, acted upon Henry's comment that the death of Richard would ease his fears.

King Henry is fearful that the Percys will succeed in deposing him, perhaps so as to install as king the lord Edmund Mortimer, whom Richard II had named as his heir. Henry refuses to give in to Hotspur's demand that the captive Mortimer be ransomed, citing the belief that Mortimer had purposely led his soldiers to their deaths at the hands of the Welsh despite Hotspur's insistence that he had fought honorably. This is one of several instances when the spectator may not be sure whether the king truly believes something or is simply demonstrating that he believes it for political purposes. In this case, Hotspur then tells his father and uncle—with no evidence of willful deceit—that he observed the king "trembling" at the mention of Mortimer's name; as such, spectators likely believe that the king indeed fears the potential popularity of Mortimer.

As word spread of the Percys' intended rebellion, Henry summons his son, whom he entreats to leave behind his life of misdeeds. The king in fact speaks at length about the political benefits he reaped by not allowing the common people to grow too familiar with him. This profession of personal belief helps explain why even the play's spectators will not be privileged enough to see the king's most profound depths. Later, in the course of the battle, spectators may be left with the impression that the king is somewhat cowardly, in that he has dressed several men in royal garb to confuse the rebels. Interestingly, Shakespeare gives no indication as to how valiantly the king fought, while in *Shakespeare's Kings*, John Julius Norwich writes, "There can, however, be no doubt that the King—who, it must be remembered, was still only thirty-six—fought with exemplary courage throughout." Shakespeare perhaps wished to shine the spotlight most pointedly on Prince Henry rather than on the king.

Overall, Henry's character ever remains mysterious, as he leaves much unsaid or only hinted at; also, the spectator does not gain insight into Henry through a soliloquy at any point. Different actors might easily play Henry's character with varying tones of sincerity, such as during his heart-to-heart talk with his son, when his words and sentiments could be presented as utterly honest or as calculated toward bringing about Prince Henry's reformation. Henry's voicing the suspicion that his son might even fight against him along with the Percys seems to force Prince Henry's hand, as at that point the son has little choice but to offer assurance that he will become the man his father needs him to become. From the play in print, Shakespeare's indirect characterization of Henry forces the spectator to understand the king based on what others say about him and on his actions. Through this indirect characterization, Henry generally comes across as a Machiavellian character, using whatever means he deems appropriate, whether straightforward or manipulative, to achieve his political goals.

Henry, Prince of Wales

Known as Prince Hal and called Harry by his father, King Henry IV, Hal is a high-spirited youth who provokes his father's anger and disapproval by associating with common criminals, most notably with Falstaff. Hal regains his father's trust when he vows to change his ways, and he fully gains his father's favor when he both saves his father's life and bests his rival, Hotspur, in battle.

Hal's motivation to behave the way he does—first irresponsibly participating in illegal activities and tarnishing his reputation as a nobleman and prince, then later undergoing a radical transformation that proves so impressive that Henry allows him to command troops in warfare—is a subject of much debate. Many critics have argued that Hal's motives are Machiavellian: that his political ambitions are such that he can coldly use Falstaff, for whom he has no true affection, to make his transformation from careless youth to responsible prince seem dramatic, deeply impressive, and well timed. Other critics agree about Hal's calculations but argue that he establishes a true friendship with Falstaff for the purpose of gaining knowledge about the people he will one day rule. Still other critics believe that Hal was genuinely enamored of Falstaff from the beginning, in that the latter served as a favorable alternative to his own father, and that the prince's transformation is not staged but quite sincere. Finally, some believe that Hal has to deal with two conflicting natures within himself—the carefree youth and the ambitious prince. His ambition is strong and he understands his responsibilities as heir, such that he manages to suppress his easy-going nature in order to assume those responsibilities.

The reader can perhaps deduce some of Shakespeare's intentions regarding Hal's character by examining the ways in which he did not strictly follow the historical record. To begin with, much of the prince's boisterous youth was passed on as legend, not as fact, and the account of Hal's early life that Shakespeare used, *The Famous Victories of Henry V*, was a dramatic account that did not claim to be accurate itself. That anonymous play actually featured a more sudden, unexpected conversion of the prince than Shakespeare presents. Thus, Shakespeare endows his Hal with a greater degree of self-reflection than his unknown predecessor. On the other hand, in real life, the prince had fought in several military engagements over the few years before the battle at Shrewsbury; at one point he even advanced into Wales alongside Hotspur, and he was occupied in Wales, not in the Boar's Head tavern, when word reached him of the Percy's rebellion. Overall, then, Shakespeare develops a

Prince Henry whose conversion is more dramatic than history would indicate, but is not exaggerated.

With respect to the battle at Shrewsbury itself, the real-life prince was not known to have offered to fight Hotspur one on one so as to avoid a full battle. The prince likely did not personally save his father from imminent death, with Norwich noting, "Holinshed goes no further than to say that the prince 'holpe his father like a lustie yoong gentleman.'" Also, Holinshed only indirectly suggests that Hal himself killed Hotspur. In adding these three aspects to his plot, Shakespeare endows the prince with inflated degrees of courtesy and heroic valor. One last passage that perhaps reveals much about Shakespeare's intention is the one in which Vernon describes the prince to Hotspur as "gallantly armed," as rising "like feathered Mercury," and as "an angel" riding atop "a fiery Pegasus." In his essay entitled "The Protean Prince Hal," Matthew Wikander notes, "The taming of Pegasus was considered in Renaissance iconography to be an allegory of self-mastery, triumph over the appetites, and statesmanship." Thus, in sum, the reader may justifiably conclude that the prince should be viewed in a favorable light —if he is calculating or cunning, he is at least also benevolent, honest, and courageous.

John of Lancaster

The younger brother of Prince Henry, John, who in real life was only thirteen during the battle at

Shrewsbury, fights valiantly there and earns his brother's esteem.

Richard le Scroop, Archbishop of York

The archbishop is a supporter of the Percy rebellion against King Henry IV. The archbishop's brother, a supporter of King Richard II, was executed at the behest of Henry.

Sir Michael

Sir Michael is a follower of the Archbishop of York.

Edmund Mortimer, Earl of March

Edmund Mortimer is Lady Percy's brother, and rightful heir of the deceased Richard II. (For this character, Shakespeare in fact conflated two real-life Edmund Mortimers, one of whom was captured by Glendower, the other of whom was the nephew of the first and was Richard's heir.) Mortimer marries Glendower's daughter, effectively allying the Welshman with the Percys. Mortimer's inability to communicate with his Welsh-speaking wife serves to highlight the distances between men and women in the play.

Lady Mortimer

Glendower's daughter and Mortimer's wife, she speaks and understands only Welsh, while her husband comprehends only English. Her portrayal as relatively exotic serves to heighten the perceived psychological distance between the men and the women of the play.

Henry Percy, Earl of Northumberland

Hotspur's father, Northumberland was one of the original supporters of Henry IV, assisting in allowing the exiled Bolingbroke to return to England. Northumberland and his family rebel against the king because they believe he has turned his back on those who helped him gain power. Northumberland fails to assist in the rebel cause, however, in that he falls ill before the battle at Shrewsbury.

Sir Henry Percy

Known as Hotspur and also as Harry, Hotspur is a passionate, hot-headed youth who regards honor, chivalry, and bravery in battle above all else. With his father and uncle, Hotspur plots a rebellion against King Henry IV. While the real-life Henry Percy, at around forty years of age during the battle at Shrewsbury, was in fact older even than Henry IV himself, Shakespeare made him a younger man, such that Hotspur and Hal are agemates and their rivalry is intensified.

While Hotspur's sense of honor is generally seen as admirable, his obsession with it may also be seen as foolish and deadly; even when the odds have fully turned against the rebels, he announces, "Doomsday is near; die all, die merrily," but he does not consider avoiding the military engagement so as to save his men's lives. Shakespeare seems to tie Hotspur's obsession with honor to an exaggerated, if not absolute, masculinity, as evidenced by his conversations with his wife. In the first, when Hotspur has just read the letter from an anonymous lord and the impending rebellion is foremost in his mind, Lady Percy proves utterly unable to draw out his softer sentiments. She notes that even in his sleep he thinks (and speaks) only of courage and war; when she attempts to turn his thoughts to his love for her, he momentarily denies that he loves her at all rather than concede the argument. Only when he is on horseback, geared toward battle by his activity, will he allow himself to admit his affection. In their second conversation, Lady Percy quite accurately characterizes him as being wholly "governed by humors." When he disparages the Welshwoman's singing and she tells him to "be still," he remarks that he will not do so because stillness is "a woman's fault." Indeed, Hotspur seems compelled to always remain in motion.

In his dealings with other men, then, Hotspur conversely comes across as childishly unable to control his passions in several scenes. When he, his father, and his uncle are discussing the best course of action after meeting with the king, he repeatedly digresses into angry tirades, and when the rebels are discussing the potential division of the nation he cannot help but express his doubts regarding Glendower's magical powers. Indeed, he largely fails to mature or evolve over the course of the play, and in certain respects this leads to his extinction.

Lady Percy

Hotspur's witty and affectionate wife, Lady Percy proves her worth as the temperamental Hotspur's mate; she chides him for being emotionally withdrawn and even threatens to break one of his fingers if he fails to communicate with her.

Thomas Percy, Earl of Worcester

Worcester is Hotspur's uncle. Like his brother, Northumberland, Worcester questions King Henry IV's treatment of his former supporters. Worcester is held to be largely responsible for the uprising, as Westmorland refers to him as "malevolent to [the King] in all aspects." Indeed, Worcester declines to communicate Henry's final offer of pardons to the rebels, as he believes that Henry will never again trust them and will certainly attempt to dispose of them sometime in the future.

Peto

Peto is one of Falstaff's thieving companions.

Edward Poins

Poins is a companion of Hal's and Falstaff's; he is referred to simply as Ned. Poins draws Hal into the Gad's Hill jest, leading to Falstaff's comical tall tale about the robbing of the thieves. In that Poins and Hal together mock Falstaff, Poins serves to illuminate the distinctions between the prince and the paunchy old soldier.

Mistress Quickly

The hostess of the Boar's Head Tavern, she is portrayed as fairly slow witted, understanding few of Falstaff's lewd comments and sexual references.

Sir Richard Vernon

Vernon is a nobleman and rebel.

Honor

In *Henry IV, Part One*, different characters signify various distinct versions of honor. Hotspur's honor is achieved through warfare, and is marked by chivalrous action, family loyalty, and patriotism; to a certain extent, Hotspur's aggressive pursuit of honor shows his disregard for human life. Hotspur's conception of honor is partly portrayed as an outdated one, losing its relevance as early as the action of the play, at the turn of the fifteenth century. As such, Hal's view accords more with what Shakespeare's audiences would have been familiar with and approving of. Indeed, scholars have cited certain Elizabethan sources as containing references to the type of honor represented by Hal, which might also be labeled "courtesy." Hal's honor is demonstrated largely by his loyalty to his father, to his country, and to his fellow man. Hal's sense of honor is more humane than Hotspur's in that Hal does not seek warfare but fights when necessary; with the battle at Shrewsbury imminent, Hal even seeks to avert the thousands of deaths to come at the possible expense of his own life, offering to engage in one-on-one combat with the pre-eminent Hotspur.

A virtual negation of the importance of honor is presented by Falstaff, as he comments on the futility of possessing honor and fully demonstrates that he has no interest in honestly attaining it. Perhaps even more than Hal, Falstaff recognizes the human cost of honor, and he refuses to let that cost prove to be his own life. The short soliloquy Falstaff offers before the Shrewsbury battle demonstrates his ambivalence to the prideful concept of honor: "Who hath it? He that died o' Wednesday. Doth he feel it? No. Doth he hear it? No. 'Tis insensible, then? Yea, to the dead. But will it not live with the living? No. Why? Detraction will not suffer it. Therefore I'll none of it. Honor is a mere scutcheon." That is, since the disparagement of others is enough to destroy it—since the attainment of honor depends on the opinions of others—he has no interest in it; as such, he can retain the utmost control of his own life. Thus, while Falstaff will gain no favor with the community through honorable acts, he provides for himself a maximum degree of self-determination.

Fathers and Sons

The father-son relationship is loosely configured in three different ways in *Henry IV, Part One*: as between King Henry and Hal, between King Henry and Hotspur, and between Falstaff and Hal. Through the play's earlier acts, Henry expresses more than once his admiration for Hotspur, especially in contrast to his disappointment with Hal. Henry goes so far as to call Hotspur "the theme of honor's tongue"—thus aligning Hotspur's and Henry's high regard for honor—and to declare that "riot and dishonor stain the brow" of his own son. He even wishes that "some night-tripping fairy" had switched the two men at birth, such that Hotspur would in fact have been his son.

Still, the king does not personally treat Hotspur with any particular respect, such as in the discussion about Hotspur's prisoners; the spectator might expect as much from so practiced a politician. King Henry instead focuses his fatherly energy on his own son, desperately hoping that his instruction will bring about the youth's reformation. The interview between the two in the third act is perhaps indicative of why Hal had felt a need to stray from his father in the first place: the king primarily wishes to mold his son to be a good king, allowing little room for the kind of self-exploration that Hal demonstrates a need for.

Thus, in accord with his desire for a degree of self-determination, Hal ends up turning to Falstaff, who explicitly teaches Hal very little. Rather, Falstaff is constantly providing Hal with entertainment and, perhaps most importantly, with friendship and love. Valerie Traub argues that in this capacity, Falstaff is in fact filling a maternal role, not a paternal one. She observes that Falstaff is presented as effeminate in that he lacks the masculine inclination toward the pursuit of honor and the personal test of battle. (She notes that his name can be regarded as "false-staff," suggesting a negation of a phallic symbol.) In psychological terms, then, Traub views Hal's outgrowing his attachment to Falstaff and turning toward his father as parallel to the process whereby any son must outgrow his exclusive attachment to his mother.

Role Playing

Closely linked to the multiple father-son relationships in *Henry IV, Part One* is the theme of role playing. This link is most evident in the scene where Falstaff assists Hal in preparing to speak with his father by impersonating King Henry. In this scene, after Falstaff presents a speech similar to the one the king will indeed produce, he and Hal exchange a number of comical comments with respect to Hal's association with Falstaff. The dialogue features two very significant moments: First, Hal "deposes" Falstaff, switching roles with him, foreshadowing Hal's actual transferring of his filial feelings away from Falstaff. Second, in portraying his father—thus anticipating the time when he will indeed be king—he confirms that he will indeed "banish plump Jack" even if it means banishing "all the world." (In *Henry IV, Part Two*, Hal becomes King Henry V and indeed informs Falstaff that he will no longer associate with him.)

Such role playing is perhaps the only way Hal could have communicated to Falstaff what he knew the future would hold for them, because, as David Bevington observes, Falstaff is inextricably immersed in the world of role playing: "Play-acting to him is more than a means of captivating Hal. It is the essence of the temptation he lays before Hal." Bevington adds, "This kind of all-consuming play world offers an invaluable critique and means of testing reality, but as an end in itself it becomes an escape." Thus, while Hal has learned much about himself by sharing in the type of role playing that Falstaff encourages, he understands that he must eventually cease trivial role playing so as to inhabit the real-life roles of prince and, later, of king.

Topics for Further Study

- The failures and successes of political and revolutionary movements often depend upon the qualities of their leaders. Research the rebellion depicted in *Henry IV, Part One* and one other rebellion from English history. Then, write an essay comparing and contrasting the personalities of Hotspur and of the leader of the rebellion you chose to research. Make reference to

Shakespeare's portrayal of Hotspur in the course of your discussion.

- Characters in Shakespeare's play make frequent reference to lions and to hares. Research the symbolism that would have been associated with these two animals in Elizabethan times and write an essay on the significance of these references.

- The pursuit of honor is a major theme in this play. Think of times in your own life when you have made decisions based on the pursuit of honor. Present a report to the class in which you discuss one situation where you made a decision that you believe was honorable and one situation where you made a decision that you believe was dishonorable. Where appropriate, compare your actions to the actions of characters from *Henry IV, Part One*.

- King Henry IV is given no soliloquies in this play, despite the fact that his name constitutes the title. Write a soliloquy for King Henry IV, in which he reveals what you believe his innermost thoughts might be. As the king always speaks in verse, your soliloquy should likewise be in verse. Indicate where in the play your soliloquy would be placed.

- While rulership was almost strictly hereditary in England in medieval times, it is almost never so in the United States of America. Nevertheless, George W. Bush went on to become president eight years after his father, George H. W. Bush, was president. Write an essay examining the lives of the two Bush presidents alongside the lives of Henry IV and Henry V. Include within your essay passages from Shakespeare's play that bear relevance to the two Bush presidents.

- Read a play published before 1600 that could be classified as a morality play. In a report, discuss the various ways in which *Henry IV, Part One* is similar to, and is different from, the morality play you chose to read.

In a more symbolic strain, commentators have noted how Hal's ability to play different roles at will is characteristic of the evolution of English society from the Medieval period into the Renaissance. R. A. Martin takes care in phrasing the course of this societal change: "Men come to be seen as actors rather than as mere performers—men *play* roles rather than *embody* them." That is, rather than simply exhibiting himself before a crowd as a juggler or circus performer does, a man of the new era must be able to inhabit different personae, like an actor, as appropriate to different circumstances. Hotspur, Martin notes, meets with much difficulty in developing genuine relationships and in stepping back from his hyper masculine pursuit of honor: "He only feels comfortable with his role as a warrior, not his role as a husband. In the end he forsakes single combat with his wife in favor of single combat with Prince Hal." In that Hal emerges from this combat victorious, the spectator can understand that he is the better adapted to the role-playing demanded by the changing times.

Heavenly Bodies

Shakespeare makes extensive reference to heavenly bodies throughout *Henry IV, Part One*, in two contexts in particular. The first context highlights the opposition between sun and moon, or between day and night. In the first tavern scene, Falstaff refers to thieves as "Diana's foresters" and "minions of the moon," in that they carry out their thievery at night. Hal replies to these comments by noting that in being governed by the moon, "the fortune of us, that are the moon's men, doth ebb and flow like the sea"; that is, the moon is associated with secrecy and inconstancy. At the end of this scene, Hal informs the spectator that he intends to soon "imitate the sun" by emerging from behind the "base contagious clouds" that have been obscuring his true self from the world. Thus, in maturing, Hal, the king's son, will prove himself as permanent as the sun in the sky.

A second context is revealed most prominently in the passage where King Henry is beseeching Prince Henry to reform himself. The king repeatedly invokes images of heavenly bodies: soon after his return from exile, when he was gaining a good reputation he was wondered at "like a comet"; in time, he "stole all courtesy from heaven"; and ultimately, he refers to the "sun-like majesty" he certainly believes he possesses. His speaking in such grand terms reflects not only the obvious gravity of the situation—success or defeat in civil war may hinge on the prince's actions—but also the king's conception of how life in England truly does revolve around him, as the world was believed to revolve around the sun. The kingship had indeed been historically perceived as a divine position, such that the concepts of God, heaven, sun, and king were all very closely linked. While an Elizabethan viewer may have taken such royal and astronomical associations for granted, the modern reader may find them instructive about the perceptions of the era.

Style

Prose vs. Verse

Shakespeare's alternate uses of prose and verse are more pronounced in *Henry IV, Part One* than in many of his other plays. In the world of the tavern, Falstaff's world, prose is spoken, and in the world of the court, also identified as the historical world, verse is spoken. Hal, at ease in both worlds, uses the appropriate language when in the tavern or at court, except for his tavern soliloquy in the first act, which he delivers in verse. Also, when Hal leaves Eastcheap for the last time, at the end of the third act, he finishes his speech with a rhyming couplet, and Falstaff responds likewise. Aside from this couplet, Falstaff speaks only in prose, demonstrating his complete opposition to the courtly world. Hotspur, who embodies honor and a certain historical courtliness, perhaps speaks the best verse in the play, with his speeches especially well metered and ornamented with elaborate phrasings. *Richard II*, the preceding play in the Lancaster tetralogy, bears not a single line of prose, such that the fairly even split between prose and verse in *Henry IV, Part One* is especially apparent to a modern reader comparing the two plays. Bevington observes that this marked difference characterizes "the shift in language from the medieval and ceremonial speech of *Richard II* to the Renaissance and practical speech of *[Part] I, Henry*

Oaths

The extensive use of oaths throughout the play can be seen as reflective of the means by which Henry IV originally obtained the kingship. Speaking to the king before the battle at Shrewsbury, Worcester reminds him, "And you did swear that oath at Doncaster, / That you did nothing purpose 'gainst the state." Worcester goes on to note how the king later dismissed that oath in gaining the favor of the people and ultimately usurping the crown. With respect to these events, Bevington states, "King Henry, having instigated the idea that a king's word lacks sacred ranking, must suffer the consequences: for him, the oath as a locutionary act can no longer be binding." Indeed, oaths are produced and contradicted repeatedly by many of the play's characters, especially Falstaff. By highlighting these instances of dishonesty, Shakespeare highlights the way Henry ushered into history a new era of political ambiguity.

The Morality Play

In devising the plot of *Henry IV, Part One*, Shakespeare drew to a fair extent on the established tradition of the morality play, as David Bevington discusses at length. Morality plays were typically far less subtle than Shakespeare's works, with characters bearing names such as Idleness and Gluttony, and with plots often featuring sudden conversions rather than complex characterizations. In *The Famous Victories of Henry V*, the anonymous author attributes just such a conversion to Hal. Tavern scenes were also common in morality plays, as they provided fitting locales in which the darker, more irresponsible sides of characters could be revealed. The morality play is most pointedly evoked when Hal describes Falstaff as "that reverend Vice, that grey iniquity, that father ruffian, that vanity in years." Indeed, the Vice was a common morality play character, ever intentionally tempting protagonists to adopt sinful ways. Bevington notes that while Falstaff is not presented as explicitly evil, as the Vice was typically portrayed, the two share "a double image of witty *bonhomie* and incorrigibility, thereby giving rise to an inextricable mixture of farce and high moral seriousness."

Aside from the tavern setting and the Vice-like character of Falstaff, the overall framework of *Henry IV, Part One* also largely reflects the worlds of virtuous and dissipated alternatives presented in moral drama. Shakespeare constantly shifts his scenes from the world of the king and the various lords to the world of thieves and common people, highlighting for spectators the contrasting natures of those two worlds. Bevington notes that the tableau presented when Hal stands over the two apparently dead bodies of Hotspur and Falstaff is a fitting symbolic end to Hal's evolution: both of his possible extreme choices—that of obsession with honor and that of utter indifference to it—have perished, and he has successfully chosen a moderate path between those two choices. Also, Falstaff's rising to bear the dead Hotspur on his back is reminiscent of morality play scenes in which the devil carries a man of the world off to hell. Overall, Bevington concludes, "the legacy of moral choice expressed concretely through the pairing and contrasting of characters is central to *[Part] I Henry IV*'s dramatic structure."

The Middle Ages vs. the Renaissance

Many critics have noted that *Henry IV, Part One* symbolically documents the evolution of English society from the Middle Ages, also referred to as medieval times, into the Renaissance. The Middle Ages are generally seen as having ended sometime in the fifteenth century throughout the world, with the English Renaissance beginning around the 1520s. Thus, Shakespeare was writing of medieval times from well within the Renaissance period (also called the early modern period), and an awareness of that cultural shift permeates the play, especially as it is viewed in the context of the Lancastrian tetralogy. That tetralogy, also known as Shakespeare's second tetralogy and as the Henriad, includes the preceding *Richard II*, and the ensuing *Henry IV, Part Two*, and *Henry V*.

This monumental cultural shift from medieval to modern world is demonstrated in *Henry IV, Part One* in a wide variety of ways. Bevington notes that changing religious and theological views played a substantial role in the shift, as provoked in part by the Reformation. The Reformation began in Europe around 1517, when Martin Luther's objections to the absolutist authority of the Roman Catholic Church led to the rise of Protestantism. In general, then,

Europeans began to place less emphasis on divine command—traditionally, the English monarchs claimed that authority was vested in them by God himself—and more on the acts of individual men. This did not entail disbelief in God but simply a greater admission of human impact on the world. Bevington writes, "Renaissance humanism … reconciled a belief in God as the ordainer of a rational and good design with an increased awareness of secondary causes in history attributable to behaviour of men." In *Henry IV, Part One*, Henry negated the popular perception that English royalty derived their power from God because he himself was not a descendant of previous kings; he was a usurper. Nevertheless, Shakespeare does not offer an unqualified endorsement of either King Henry and his supporters, or of the rebels, as he might have done if he himself had believed that, say, God must have been supporting the ultimate victors. Rather, as Bevington declares, Shakespeare "gives us a whole range of possible answer to questions of rebellion and loyalty in a kind of empirical openness that is characteristic of the best political theorists of the age."

Some critics have seen the inception of Renaissance ideals as especially evident with regard to gendered constructs within and between characters; this notion is closely linked with the theme of role playing. R. A. Martin begins his discussion in "Metatheater, Gender, and Subjectivity in *Richard II* and *Henry IV*, Part I," by describing the cultural shift in question as "a movement from a static, ceremonial view of human life to a dramatic and historical one." With respect to the dramatic aspect, women in particular are keen to demonstrate their individuality and devise roles for themselves within the Renaissance world. Martin notes that in *Richard II*, "Women are thoroughly assimilated to the existing values and hierarchies of a monolithic patriarchal state even when they might appear to be criticizing them." In *Henry IV, Part One*, on the other hand, as demonstrated by the willful, aggressive Lady Percy, "Women are no longer benign extensions of the patriarchal social order: they are autonomous, self-motivated, and problematic." In that women are portrayed as thus asserting themselves, men must come to terms with the broadened emphasis on "personal relationships and life as opposed to honor and heroic death." This shift in emphasis proves most difficult for Hotspur to deal with. Martin concludes with regard to the ultimate demise of the chivalric, honor-seeking Hotspur, "He does not solve the problems posed by a heterogenous and sexually differentiated world … and he illustrates the extent to which masculine subjectivity is being restructured."

David Bevington appropriately sums up the cultural shift Shakespeare demonstrates in this play: "The ideal world of what ought to be gives way to the unselected, chaotic flow of history, to contingency and temporality." He further speaks of "the destruction of a divinely sanctioned culture only to be replaced by cunning and political expediency." Matthew H. Wikander goes on to note that Shakespeare had a number of models of such political intelligence in Elizabethan times—most notably, Queen Elizabeth herself, as well as the Earl of Essex, who was long rumored to be a potential mate for the queen.

Compare & Contrast

- **1400s:** Political leaders do not necessarily act with the intent of shaping public opinion about themselves. As asserted by the character of King Henry in *Henry IV, Part One*, Richard II, his predecessor, fully engaged himself with the common people, frequently appearing before them and responding to their inquiries and accusations alike. Henry IV, on the other hand, limited public access to him under the belief that the less people understood of him, the more he would retain an aura of elevated majesty.

  1600s: Queen Elizabeth, nearing the end of her reign, has proven a master at shaping the public's perception of her. Among other image-defining acts, in 1588 she gave a speech before English troops at Tilbury while dressed in a coat of armor and riding on horseback. Russ

McDonald notes in his *Bedford Companion to Shakespeare*, "Leaving ministers and lackeys to censure, to punish, to refuse, she dwelt on the affirmative themes of unity, forgiveness, and affection for her people, and doing so with graciousness and majesty, she thereby won their hearts."

Today: The political consideration and manipulation of public opinion is ubiquitous. In England and America alike, politicians nearly always employ image consultants or, at the very least, assistants who pay particular attention to the public perception of their image and how that perception can be shaped. Politicians often prove unsuccessful because they fail to project a likable and genuine personality; that is, politicians who are not also decent actors may have difficulty getting elected.

- **1400s:** The kingship is seen as directly connected to divine authority, with Roman Catholicism being the official state religion. Thus, treason, or rebellion against the state, and heresy, or rebellion against the church, are often equated. Bevington discusses how Shakespeare's portrayal of the characters in *Henry IV, Part One* reflect an awareness of this connection: "Lancastrian supporters of Bolingbroke and his son reflect the Lancastrian myth that Providence overthrew Richard II and favoured his successor; Yorkist supporters … reflect the Yorkist myth branding the Henrys as usurpers and regicides who deserve providential punishment in the form of civil rebellion."

1600s: Elizabeth I, following in the footsteps of Henry VIII, makes England a Protestant nation rather than a Catholic nation; in 1570, Elizabeth herself is officially excommunicated by the Pope. In that Protestantism features a rejection of papal authority, a natural consequence is that divine authority is also farther removed from the English monarch. Thus, while religion continued to play a significant role in the actions of heads of state, humans were seen as possessing greater degrees of control and authority.

Today: While England retains a state-sponsored church and incorporates church teachings and authority into schooling and political bodies in certain respects, political leaders such as the prime minister are not also considered religious leaders. Meanwhile, religion and politics are fully separated by law in America, with intersections such as those between prayer and schools, between the Ten Commandments and federal law, and between religious and secular views of contraception provoking widespread debate.

- **1400s:** The future Henry V reportedly spends much of his youth fraternizing with thieves and scoundrels; however, public awareness of his activities is limited, and since he will bear himself regally, his past will not affect his rule as king.
  1600s: James I has been king of Scotland since he was a year old and as such has led a highly supervised life; nevertheless, his manner is crude, and he will prove less respected than his predecessor, Elizabeth.
  Today: Members of the British royal family still sometimes come under intense public criticism for poor behavior.

The Character of Sir John Falstaff

The way Shakespeare formulated the character of Falstaff, who is widely understood to have been based on the real-life personage of one Sir John Oldcastle, reveals much about religious and political currents of the era. The true Oldcastle was a devout Protestant who heralded the doctrines of the fourteenth-century theologian John Wycliffe, a critic of the excesses of the Catholic Church. Oldcastle was indeed at one time a friend of the man who became Henry V, but he was nevertheless ultimately burned to death as a heretic, or one who contradicts church doctrine. Both Oldcastle and Wycliffe, then, emphasized personal salvation, especially as obtained through close reading of the Bible, over the institutionalized salvation of the church.

As Tom McAlindon describes him in "Perfect Answers: Religious Inquisition, Falstaffian Wit," Oldcastle was "a reformed sinner who publicly confessed that in his youth he offended grievously in pride, wrath, gluttony, covetousness, and lechery." Oldcastle went on, however, to thoroughly familiarize himself with the verses and teachings of the Bible. When he went on trial, for both treason and heresy, he responded intelligently, even wittily, to the various accusations put forth by the team of theologians that interviewed him. That is, while his religious conceptions were ridiculed and condemned by those in power, he was without doubt a learned, respectable man in his own right with a thoroughly moral conception of God. What

McAlindon finds most interesting about Shakespeare's portrayal is that he did not simply "caricature Oldcastle's biblical babbling" and create a wholly despicable character; rather, Shakespeare's parody "metamorphosed the object of its mockery into something beguilingly attractive and even admirable." Falstaff is generally perceived as both whimsically and genuinely witty in his responses to accusations regarding his character and in his discourses regarding concepts such as honor and courage. Thus, this partly belittling, partly respectful depiction of Falstaff perhaps reflects not only Shakespeare's personal open-mindedness but also the increasing respect for subjective interpretations that was one aspect of the Renaissance era.

Critical Overview

Henry IV, Part One is considered to be one of the more controversial and popular of Shakespeare's histories, due to its political and moral implications as well as to the fascinating nature of the characters struggling for power in the play. Increasingly, criticism on *Henry IV, Part One* has shifted from an emphasis on character studies and the historical sources which Shakespeare drew on to define his characters and plot to an emphasis on the language, structure, and deeper psychological truths evident in the play. The debate over the exact relationship between the two parts of Henry IV intensified during the twentieth century, although an understanding of the conjectures on this topic is not necessary to understand and enjoy either play.

Samuel Johnson, the renowned eighteenth-century Shakespearean scholar, discussed both the first and second parts of Shakespeare's plays revolving around King Henry IV. As quoted by Howard Staunton in *The Complete Illustrated Shakespeare*, he noted, "Perhaps no author has ever in two plays afforded so much delight." Regarding Shakespeare's craftsmanship, he wrote, "The incidents are multiplied with wonderful fertility of invention, and the characters diversified with the utmost nicety of discernment, and the profoundest skill in the nature of man." Johnson had the most to say about the "unimitated, unimitable Falstaff," eventually concluding, "The moral to be drawn from this representation is, that no man is more dangerous than he that, with a will to corrupt, hath the power to please; and that neither wit nor honesty ought to think themselves safe with such a companion, when they see Henry seduced by Falstaff."

David Bevington similarly connotes a positive perception of the play: "The greatness of *Henry IV, Part I* is witnessed by its undiminished popularity in both performance and reading, and by an equally undiminished critical debate about its structure, themes, language, and characterization." He goes on to cite the wide array of topics over which critics have met with disagreement, such as the actual virtuousness of Hal, the extent to which Falstaff presents himself genuinely, and whether Shakespeare was supportive of one side of the rebellion or the other. Bevington asserts, "These issues are illuminated by striking motifs and images, including those of vocation and recreation, the redeeming of time, bodily illness and wounding, commercial exchange and thievery, sun and moon, lion and hare, Scriptural iteration and parody." Indeed, the play is so rich with various modes of metaphorical imagery that few critical treatments have even attempted to discuss them comprehensively.

Over the years, of course, critical treatments of Shakespeare's plays have delved ever deeper into the abstract notions exemplified therein. In the course of her own highly complex critical essay entitled "Prince Hal's Falstaff: Positioning

Psychoanalysis and the Female Reproductive Body," Valerie Traub summarily notes, "Psychoanalytic criticism of the Henriad has tended to perceive Prince Hal's developmental problem as a choice between two fathers: a biological father, King Henry IV, standing for conviction, duty, and control, yet burdened by his guilty acquisition of the crown; and a father substitute, Falstaff, whose hedonism, lawlessness, and wit provide an attractive, if temporary, alternative." Traub herself alters this paradigm somewhat in presenting Falstaff as essentially maternal, rather than paternal.

Sources

Bennett, Robert B., "Hal's Crisis of Timing," in *Cahiers Elisabethans*, No. 13, April 1978, pp. 15-23.

Bevington, David, "Introduction," in *Henry IV, Part 1*, by William Shakespeare, Oxford University Press, 1987, pp. 1-122.

Bueler, Lois, "Falstaff in the Eye of the Beholder," in *Essays in Literature*, Vol. 1, No. 1, January 1973, pp. 1-12.

Callahan, E. F., "Lyric Origins of the Unity of *1 Henry IV*," *Costerus*, Vol. 3, 1972, pp. 9-22.

Cohen, Derek, "The Rite of Violence in *1 Henry IV*," *Shakespeare Survey*, Vol. 38, 1985, pp. 77-84.

Cox, Gerard H. "'Like a Prince Indeed': Hal's Triumph of Honor in *1 Henry IV*," in *Pageantry in the Shakespearean Theater*, edited by David M. Bergeron, University of Georgia Press, 1985, pp. 130-49.

Cruttwell, Patrick, *The Shakespearean Moment and Its Place in the Poetry of the Seventeenth Century*, Chatto & Windus, 1954, pp. 27-8.

Dickinson, Hugh, "The Reformation of Prince Hal," in *Shakespeare Quarterly*, Vol. 12, No. 1, Winter 1961, pp. 33-46.

Goddard, Harold C., "Henry IV," in *The Meaning of Shakespeare*, University of Chicago Press, 1951, pp. 161-214.

Gross, Alan Gerald, "The Justification of Prince Hal," in *Texas Studies in Literature and Language*, Vol. 10, No. 1, Spring 1978, pp. 27-35.

Humphreys, A. R. "Shakespeare's Political Justice in *Richard II* and *Henry IV*," in *Stratford Papers on Shakespeare*, edited by B. W. Jackson, Gage, 1965, pp. 30-50.

Lawlor, John, "Appearance and Reality," in *Tragic Sense in Shakespeare*, Chatto & Windus, 1960, pp. 17-44.

Martin, R. A., "Metatheater, Gender, and Subjectivity in *Richard II* and *Henry IV*, Part I," in *Comparative Drama*, Vol. 23, No. 3, Fall 1989, pp. 255-64.

McAlindon, Tom, "Perfect Answers: Religious Inquisition, Falstaffian Wit," in *Shakespeare Survey*, Vol. 54, 2001, pp. 100-07.

McDonald, Russ, "The Monarchs," in *The Bedford Companion to Shakespeare*, 2nd ed., Bedford/St. Martin's, 2001, p. 313.

Morgann, Maurice, "An Essay on the Dramatic Character of Sir John Falstaff," in *Shakespearian Criticism*, edited by Daniel A. Fineman, Clarendon Press, 1972, p. 444.

Norwich, John Julius, *Shakespeare's Kings*, Scribner, 1999.

Reno, Raymond, "Hotspur: The Integration of Character and Theme," in *Renaissance Papers*,

April 1962, pp. 17-26.

Rogers, Carmen, "The Renaissance Code of Honor in Shakespeare's *Henry IV, Part I*," in *The Shakespeare Newsletter*, Vol. 4, No. 1, February 1954, p. 8.

Rowse, A. L., "The First Part of King Henry IV," in *Prefaces to Shakespeare's Plays*, Orbis, 1984, pp. 49-53.

Shakespeare, William, *The Complete Illustrated Shakespeare*, edited by Howard Staunton, 1858, reprint, Park Lane, 1979.

——————, *Henry IV, Part 1*, edited by David Bevington, Oxford University Press, 1987.

Siegel, Paul N., "Shakespeare and the Neo-Chivalric Cult of Honor," in *Centennial Review*, Vol. 8, 1964, pp. 39-70.

Sjoberg, Elisa, "From Madcap Prince to King: The Evolution of Prince Hal," in *Shakespeare Quarterly*, Vol. 20, No. 1, Winter 1969, pp. 11-6.

Traub, Valerie, "Prince Hal's Falstaff: Positioning Psychoanalysis and the Female Reproductive Body," in *Shakespeare Quarterly*, Vol. 40, No. 4, Winter 1989, pp. 456-74.

Vickers, Brian, *The Artistry of Shakespeare's Prose*, Methuen, 1968, pp. 1-51, 89-141.

Wikander, Matthew H., "The Protean Prince Hal," in *Comparative Drama*, Vol. 26, No. 4, Winter 1992–1993, pp. 295-311.

Wilson, John Dover, "The Political Background of

Shakespeare's Richard II and Henry IV," in *Shakespeare Jahrbuch*, Vol. 75, 1939, pp. 36-51.

—————————, *The Fortunes of Falstaff*, Cambridge University Press, 1964, p. 143.

Zeeveld, Gordon, ""Food for Powder'—'Food for Worms?'" in *Shakespeare Quarterly*, Vol. 3, 1952, pp. 249-53.

Further Reading

Bevan, Bryan, *Henry IV*, Palgrave Macmillan, 1994.

> Bevan provides a book-length treatment of the life of King Henry IV, addressing his virtues as well as his faults.

Cooper, Terry D., *Sin, Pride & Self-Acceptance: The Problem of Identity in Theology and Psychology*, InterVarsity Press, 2003.

> In a work that bears relevance to the various psychological states Hal may have experienced over the course of his life, Cooper addresses the notion of how pride can lead a person to imagine an idealized self that can be difficult to develop in actuality.

Forrest, Ian, *The Detection of Heresy in Late Medieval England*, Oxford University Press, 2005.

> Addressing the case of John Oldcastle among many others, Forrest examines the notion of heresy in England in the fourteenth and fifteenth centuries and the way it was addressed by church and state authorities.

Valente, Claire, *The Theory and Practice of Revolt in Medieval England*, Ashgate Publishing, 2003.

In this text, Valente explores the various rebellions that occurred in England from the thirteenth through the fifteenth centuries, including the one by which Henry IV rose to power as well as the one he faced from the Percys and their supporters.